Chris

SEVEN
THINGS THE
HOLY SPIRIT
WILL DO IN YOU

LoveWorld Publishing

7 Things The Holy Spirit Will Do In You

ISBN– 978-37866-1-x

Copyright © 2004 LoveWorld Publishing Ministry

BELIEVERS' LOVEWORLD INC.

a.k.a Christ Embassy

UNITED KINGDOM:
Christ Embassy Int'l Office
Loveworld Conference Centre
Cheriton High Street
Folkestone, Kent CT19 4QJ
Tel:+44(0)1303 270970
Fax:01303 274 372

USA:
Christ Embassy Int'l Office
12400 Westheimer Road,
Houston, Texas 77077
Tel:+1-281-759-5111;
    +1-281-759-6218

CANADA:
101 RossDean Drive,
Toronto, ON, Canada M9L 1S6
Tel/Fax:+1-416-746 5080

NIGERIA:
Loveworld Conference Centre
Kudirat Abiola Way,
Oregun, Ikeja, Lagos.
P.O. Box 13563 Ikeja, Lagos.
Tel:+234-802 3324 188,
+234-805 2464 131,
+234-1-892 5724

SOUTH AFRICA:
303 Pretoria Avenue
Cnr. Harley and Bram Fischer,
Randburg, Gauteng
South Africa.
Tel: +27 11 3260971;
     +27 113260972

email: cec@christembassy.org
website: www.christembassy.org

Contents

Introduction

*T*he greatest thing that God has done for us since we believed is to make His Spirit available to us. However, too many of God's people are like the 12 men in Acts chapter 19, who Paul asked, "Have you received the Holy Ghost since you believed?" and they answered him, "We have not so much as heard whether there be any Holy Ghost!"

Many Christians are completely clueless of who the Holy Spirit is. Many others who even claim to know the Holy Spirit and have Him in their lives don't know why He is in them. They have no idea what He can do with them, in them and through them.

In this book, I'll be teaching you seven vital things the Holy Spirit will do in you when He comes to dwell in you; seven things that will not happen in your life until you receive and are full of the Holy Spirit. I've already written a book on *'**Seven Things The Holy Spirit Will Do *For* You**,' but now I'll be sharing with you what He'll do ***inside*** you when He comes to abide in you.

In **Hosea 12:13**, the Bible says, **"...by a prophet the Lord brought Israel out of Egypt, and by a prophet was he preserved."**

Understand what God is saying here. He's letting you know that the way He changes your life is by sending you another human being. He will not come down Himself into your room; neither will He send an angel from heaven to change your life. Even if you saw an angel, that may not change your life. God Himself may appear to you today and your life will not change.

Introduction

What changes your life is when God sends a message to you through another human being.

In Acts 10 when an angel appeared to Cornelius, the Roman centurion, he told him to send messengers to Joppa and fetch Simon Peter who would speak words to him by which he would be saved.

In the same way, God brought Israel out of Egypt; He brought them out of their suffering, sorrow and bondage by sending them a prophet by the name of Moses. Moses delivered them from their bondage to Egypt and changed their lives.

The message that God put in Moses' mouth to speak to the children of Israel was the message that kept them alive. That was the message that gave them prosperity and success. It was the same message that established them and helped them in everything they did.

In the same way God brought Israel out of Egypt and preserved them through the prophet Moses, He has sent me to you as His prophet to give you a Word of revelation in this book that is guaranteed to change your life forever.

your life forever.

Don't take the things you're about to read or the thoughts they'll stir in you lightly. They will change your family, your finances and your health. They will change everything about your life today and your future!

This message of the Spirit will bring you light. It will change your ministry, your relationships, your job or your business. It will produce a great future for you and change your destiny forever!

You will do yourself much good to read through this book over and over until you've imbibed its message. Let the thoughts shared in it become a part of you and your daily experience. Then you'll be able to walk with the Holy Spirit in the understanding of what He is in you to do, and enjoy the fulness of the blessings of His presence in your life.

Get ready for a life-transforming encounter with the most powerful Person on earth – the Almighty Spirit of the living God!

Chapter One

Who is the Holy Spirit?

*H*ave you ever tried to ask people who or what they think the 'Holy Spirit' is. Some may tell you, "It's a cloud or smoke coming out of heaven" or "It's the anointing oil in a bottle." Others may even say, "It's my prayer handkerchief (what some call 'mantle') or "It's that influence I feel some-times that causes me to shake and speak in tongues."

Well, the Holy Spirit I'll be teaching you about is

definitely more than any of these! Oh, how I wish many more of God's children will know Him for who He really is! I will intermittently refer to Him as the Holy Ghost throughout this book, for 'Holy Spirit' and 'Holy Ghost' refer to one and the same Person.

The Holy Spirit is the third Person of the Godhead. He is the Power by which God made the whole world. The Holy Spirit, the Bible says, is the One Who garnished the heavens (Job 26:13).

When God speaks, the Holy Spirit is the One who brings it to pass. He's the Doer of the things of God. So, when God wants to do something in your life, it will have to be by the Holy Spirit. This is why you need the Holy Spirit in your life today.

Even the Lord Jesus Christ had to have the Holy Spirit. It was only after the Holy Spirit came into His life that His ministry and the miraculous began. Remember that when He was on earth, even though He was the Son of God, He didn't operate or minister as the Son of God. He operated and ministered as a man, the son of man (1 Timothy 2:5; Matthew 12:8).

The Bible says He laid aside His glory and became a man like everyone of us; and because He found Himself being fashioned as a man, He humbled Himself and became obedient even unto the death on the cross (Philippians 2:5-8).

When Jesus walked the earth, He was hungry like everyone else. He was thirsty like everyone else. He got tired and He slept like everyone else. He could be tempted like everyone else, but He never fell into any temptation (Hebrews 4:15). This was why He needed to have the Holy Spirit, because He didn't minister on earth as the Son of God even though He was the Son of God.

If you have the Holy Spirit and let Him take charge of your life, it doesn't matter what your situation is, He'll turn it around for your good. If the Holy Spirit takes over your family, your business or your health, it doesn't matter what troubles you've been experiencing or what's been going wrong, you will begin to go from strength to strength, from grace to grace, from faith to faith, from success to success and from greatness to greatness. When the Holy Spirit takes over your life, He'll drive every sickness out of your body; He'll make right everything that was wrong.

GOD'S PROMISE OF THE SPIRIT IS FOR EVERYONE

After the resurrection and ascension of the Lord Jesus Christ, His disciples (120 of them) were gathered in one accord in the upper room. Then suddenly, there came a sound from heaven as of a rushing mighty wind, and it filled the entire house where they were sitting. Cloven tongues like as of fire sat on each of them, and they were all filled with the Holy Ghost (Acts 2:1-4).

When they were all filled with the Spirit of God, they began to speak words of praise and magnify God in other tongues. Because of the way they were acting and talking, some of the people looking at them mocked them, thinking they were drunk.

But then the Bible says,

"...Peter, standing up with the eleven, lifted up his voice, and said unto them, Ye men of Judaea, and all ye that dwell at Jerusalem, be this known unto you, and hearken to my words: For these are not drunken, as ye suppose, seeing it is but the third hour of the day. But this is that which was spoken by the prophet Joel" **(Acts 2:14-16).**

The apostle Peter began to quote the prophet Joel, telling the people that what was prophesied many years ago had now come:

"And it shall come to pass in the last days, saith God, I will pour out of my Spirit upon all flesh: and your sons and your daughters shall prophesy, and your young men shall see visions, and your old men shall dream dreams: And on my servants and on my hand-maidens I will pour out in those days of my Spirit; and they shall prophesy: And

I will shew wonders in heaven above, and signs in the earth beneath; blood, and fire, and vapour of smoke: The sun shall be turned into darkness, and the moon into blood, before that great and notable day of the Lord come: And it shall come to pass, that whosoever shall call on the name of the Lord shall be saved"

Acts 2:17-21.

Then he said in **verse 38,** "... Repent, and be baptized every one of you in the name of Jesus Christ for the remission of sins, and ye shall receive the gift of the Holy Ghost."

Peter lets us know that the indwelling presence of the Holy Ghost is the gift of God to every believer. You don't have to attain to it. You don't have to 'qualify' for it. All you need is to believe in Jesus Christ. Peter also said, **"For the promise is unto you, and to your children, and to all that are afar off, even as many as the Lord our God shall call" (Acts 2:39).**

GENTILES OR JEWS

"Christ hath redeemed us from the curse of the law, being made a curse for us: for it is written, Cursed is every one that hangeth on a tree: That the blessing of Abraham might come on the Gentiles through Jesus Christ; that we might receive the promise of the Spirit through faith"
Galatians 3:13-14.

Here, the Bible lets us know Christ was made a curse for us; He was hanged on a tree. Then it tells us the reason: **"That you might receive the promise of the Holy Spirit through faith."**

Scripture speaks of two types of people: Jews and Gentiles. Gentiles, according to the Bible, are all non-Israelites. If you're American, Russian, Chinese or Nigerian, you're a gentile. No matter where you come from, as long as you're not a Jew, you're a gentile.

The Jews are the physical descendants of Abraham

but the gentiles are not related to Abraham by physical descent. Now, God says the blessing of Abraham will come on the gentiles – non-Jews – through Christ. That's the blessing that brings success, health and prosperity. It's the blessing that brings favour into your life and makes you great. That blessing comes into your life through Jesus Christ, and it includes the wonderful gift of the Holy Spirit.

God has not only made the promise of the Holy Spirit, He has actually given Him to us. It's up to us now to receive Him. But for you to receive from God, you will have to be ready to respond to Him by faith. Until you respond to God by faith, you do not receive from Him, because God is a faith-God.

Now let's look at that Scripture in **Galatians 3:14** again,

> *"That the blessing of Abraham might come on the Gentiles through Jesus Christ; that we might receive the promise of the Spirit through faith"*

There are two very important things you need to realise from this verse of Scripture. The first one is: **Whatever we must receive from God must come as an act of faith, because God is a Faith-God.**

Secondly, you must realise that **whatever blessing we receive from God can only come to us through Jesus Christ.**

RECEIVE THE HOLY SPIRIT TODAY

We need today the power of the Holy Spirit in our lives. The Holy Spirit is the Spirit of God, and until you have Him, you'll walk in darkness. It doesn't matter how educated or intelligent you are in your chosen field; it doesn't even matter how highly-placed you are in the society, until you have the Holy Ghost, your life is empty.

If you don't have the Holy Ghost, the Lord wants you to receive Him today, and I have outlined hereunder the simple steps you must take to receive

Him – **respond to God by faith** and **relate to Him through Jesus.** This means you must, first and foremost, be born again. That's the beginning of your relationship with God through Christ Jesus.

If you've not been born again, you can pray the Prayer of Salvation written below. Pray it in faith and audibly too, and you'll be saved!

> *"O Lord God, I believe in Jesus Christ the Son of the living God. I believe He died for me and I believe God raised Him from the dead. I confess with my mouth that Jesus Christ is Lord of my life from this day forward. I give my life to Jesus Christ today and open my heart by faith to receive salvation. Right now I receive eternal life into my spirit. Thank You Lord for hearing my prayer. My sins have all been washed away by the blood of Jesus. Christ now lives in me and I am free, I'm saved, I'm born again, and from today I begin to walk in*

the consciousness of my new life in Christ Jesus. Amen!"

Congratulations and welcome to the family of God! You're now a child of God. Remember that your salvation is the only qualification you require to receive the Holy Spirit. Now, you can simply ask by faith and receive Him into your spirit.

Say these words out loud, in faith, expecting to receive:

> ***"Dear Heavenly Father, I thank You for the Gift of the Holy Spirit. As Your child, I now receive Him by faith to come and dwell in my heart. I receive Him into my soul and my body. I receive Him into every fibre of my being. I am now filled with the Holy Spirit, and according to Your Word in Acts 2:4, I speak with other tongues as He gives me utterance, in the Name of the Lord Jesus Christ. Amen."***

Chapter Two

The Seven-fold Ministry Of The Holy Spirit In Your Life

*I*n **John 14:16-17**, the Lord Jesus said,

"And I will pray the Father, and he shall give you another Comforter, that he may abide with you for ever; Even the Spirit of truth; whom the world cannot receive, because it seeth him not, neither knoweth him: but ye know him; for he dwelleth with you, and shall be in you."

Here, we're shown that the Holy Spirit is the Spirit of truth – the Spirit of reality. Everything in this world is but a shadow. It's the Spirit of reality Who helps us know what is real.

> *"And I will ask the Father, and He will give you another Comforter (Counselor, Helper, Intercessor, Advocate, Stren-gthener, and Standby), that He may remain with you forever - The Spirit of Truth, Whom the world cannot receive (welcome, take to its heart), because it does not see Him or know {and} recognize Him. But you know {and} recognize Him, for He lives with you [constantly] and will be in you"*
> **John 14:16-17 Amplified.**

From the Scripture above, the Amplified Version shows us six synonyms for the word translated 'Comforter' from its Greek expression, 'Allos Parakletos.'

The word 'another' in the first place, translated

from the Greek 'Allos' is very instructive. You see, the Greek language used two words which the English commonly translated 'another' These two words are 'Heteros' and 'Allos.'

Properly expressed, 'heteros' meant another of a different kind, while 'Allos' meant another of the same kind. In referring to the Holy Spirit, Jesus called Him "allos" - 'another One of the same kind,' thus inferring the Holy Spirit to be exactly like Him. So the Holy Spirit is exactly like Jesus. He looks like Him, loves like Him, cares like Him and talks like Him. This is the Holy Spirit **sent by the Father** to be with us.

All seven words - **Comforter**, **Counselor**, **Helper**, **Intercessor**, **Advo-cate**, **Strengthener** and **Standby** – rendered from the Greek 'parakletos' help to show us the ministry of the Holy Spirit in our lives. When the Holy Spirit comes into your life, He becomes your Lawyer, Helper and Intercessor.

You know, you can have an intercessor who's praying for you from somewhere afar off or in the background. What kind of intercessor is the Holy Spirit?

He's not the kind of intercessor that's somewhere in the background; He's right there with you and in you!

The Amplified Bible gives us other words to support this. It says He's our **Advocate** and **Standby** – this means the Holy Spirit is the kind of intercessor that stands ready as our advocate or counsel for the defence. Jesus was talking about Someone Who engages our adversaries, Someone Who steps right into the middle of the heat and takes charge with us, not someone watching from somewhere in the background.

He also says the Holy Spirit is our Strengthener; so while He's taking His own steps to ensuring everything works out for our good, He's also making sure we're participating by strengthening us, for He has to function through us. When you have the Holy Ghost, weakness will not be a part of your life. No wonder Paul said, "When I am weak, then am I strong" (2 Corinthians 12:10). In other words, when he'd been bruised, battered and broken down by external factors, he was made even stronger by the power of the Holy Ghost.

The last word the Amplified Bible uses to describe the Holy Spirit is 'Standby.' He's your Standby. Think of it this way: Many companies and homes in developing countries have a 'standby generator.' When there's an outage from the main power supply, the standby generator is switched on, power is supplied and businesses and activities can continue to run normally. That's what the Holy Spirit does for you. When you run out of strength, information, ideas, options and everything else you know, there's a Standby, and He never fails, glory to God!

Our lives should always be full of joy and excitement. We've got a Helper, Comforter, Intercessor, Advocate, Counsellor, Strengthener and Standby. How could we lose? It's impos-sible!The trouble with a lot of God's children is that they're not informed of things like this, and many don't know how to operate in the realm of the Spirit.

We're not a group of people seeking help from God; we've been given a Helper. We're not alone, we have One called alongside us to help us. That's the ministry of the Holy Spirit; He's been called to go with us.

You'll be wrong to look at us born again, Spirit-filled folks and think that all you see is all there is about us. Make no mistakes about it! There's Someone Who's not only with us, He's also in us! You may not see Him with your optical eyes, but He's right there. In fact, He's more present than our adversaries.

The Psalmist calls Him a very present help in trouble (Psalm 46:1). When he said 'a very present help,' he wasn't saying there are some other helps apart from Him. He just wants us to know, by attaching the 'very' to the 'present help,' that he's referring to a definite article, in spite of the generic tone that the 'a' gives it. He could simply have said He's 'a present help' in trouble, but instead of just saying that, he strengthens it by saying He's 'a *very* present help.'

In other words, it's something you shouldn't doubt at all. You don't have to look for Him; He's a very present help in trouble. This means if you ever get into trouble, you might as well laugh and say, "Thank You Holy Spirit, I'm not alone!"

Chapter Three

He Will Give You Understanding

*T*he first thing the Holy Spirit will do in your life when He comes to dwell in you is to give you understanding. This understanding helps you receive the message of Jesus Christ. It helps you receive God's Word into your spirit. Then you won't be like people who're always asking such silly questions as: "How could Jesus have been born of a virgin?" or "How can you say that God raised Jesus from the dead?"

You no longer ask such questions because you just understand it. You simply believe Jesus was born of a virgin and was raised from the dead, because the Holy Spirit has helped you understand it.

In John 15:26, Jesus said,

"But when the Comforter is come, whom I will send unto you from the Father, even the Spirit of truth, which proceedeth from the Father, he shall testify of me."

The Holy Spirit testifies of the Lord Jesus and helps you easily believe the gospel. He gives you an understanding mind. In John 20:22, the Bible tells us that after His resurrection, Jesus stood before His disciples and breathed on them (another version says He blew on them), and when He did that, He said, "Receive the Holy Spirit."

Luke 24:45 fills us in with more details of what transpired. It lets us know that after He had said that, He opened their understanding. That's exactly what happened when He blew on them – the Holy Spirit came upon them and opened their understanding so they could receive the Word of God and understand it.

Job 32:8 (Amp.) says, "But there is [a vital force] a spirit [of intelligence] in man, and the breath of the Almighty gives men understanding."

When the Holy Spirit comes into your life, He gives you understanding so you're no longer in the dark about God's Word. Every time you hear the Word of God or study the Bible, you'll understand, because the Holy Spirit has given you understanding. Now, not only do you understand the Word of God, no matter where you are, where you go or what you do, you'll have an understanding mind and heart.

Do you remember the prayer of Solomon when he became king of Israel? The Bible says God spoke to him in a dream and asked him, "Solomon, what do you want Me to do for you?" Solomon answered and said, "Oh God, give me wisdom and an understanding heart" (1 Kings 3:9). You see, he asked God for wisdom and understanding. Now in the New Covenant, when you receive the Holy Spirit, you automatically receive understanding, The Holy Spirit is the secret of understanding, Hallelujah!

Chapter Four

He Will Bring The Anointing Into Your Life

When the Holy Spirit comes into your life and you allow Him take charge of your life, He'll bring in the anointing. The anointing of God's Spirit will come upon everything you do. Understand what it is to be anointed: the word 'anoint' comes from the Hebrew word 'MASHACH.' It means 'to smear or rub.' This signifies that the presence of God is so smeared or rubbed on you like oil, that His presence is left on you, causing divine excellence and power.

When you're anointed, you become blessed of God such that everything you touch or do prospers. To be 'blessed' means to be empowered to prosper.

The anointing is the empowerment of the Holy Spirit in our lives. It's the supernatural ability the Holy Spirit brings into our lives that cannot be explained. Suddenly, the Holy Spirit takes over your spirit and puts power within you that enables you see, think, say and do things ordinary men can't. This is the work of the anointing – it guides and leads you in everything you do.

Let me remind you at this point that Man is a spirit, he has a soul and lives in a body. Now, the real person is the spirit. With your spirit you contact the spiritual realm. Your body that you see is not the real you, it's just the house where you (your spirit) live. With your body you contact the physical realm. Your soul is what you use to function intellectually. That's where your reasoning faculties and emotions are; that's where your thinking and decision-making take place. With it you contact the mental realm. Your spirit, however, is the real you. That's the one who relates with God.

When the Holy Spirit comes to dwell in your spirit, He gives life to your spirit. Then He also anoints your spirit and your mind. He gives you understanding and blesses your spirit so that you're divinely energized from within.

In Philippians 4:13, Paul said, *"I can do all things through Christ which strengtheneth me."* When he said 'Christ' here, he wasn't talking about the Man Jesus. 'Christ' here refers to the Anointed One and His anointing. It's talking about the supernatural empowerment Jesus received that made Him the Christ when the Holy Spirit came upon Him.

Now Paul says, "I can do all things through *Christ* which strengthens me." Praise the Lord Jesus! This means when the Holy Spirit comes into your life, He will anoint you and make it possible for you to do the impossible. You will receive the ability to do things you ordinarily wouldn't be able to do. He will fill your spirit with the unction of God.

In **Acts 1:8**, Jesus said,

> *"But ye shall receive power, after that the Holy Ghost is come upon you: and ye shall be witnesses unto me both in Jerusalem, and in all Judea, and in Samaria, and unto the uttermost part of the earth."*

When the Holy Spirit comes into your life, you receive power. The word 'power' as it is used here in Acts 1:8 refers to the dynamic ability to cause changes. The Lord Jesus tells us we shall receive that dynamic ability to cause changes when the Holy Ghost comes into our lives. This means, if the circumstances of your life don't favour you, you can change them. That's what it is to be a child of God. As a child of God, you should never be disadvantaged in life or subject to circumstances!

GOD GIVES BIRTH TO GODS!

Every creature reproduces after its kind. A dog gives birth to dogs, a cat gives birth to cats, a cow gives birth to cows, a monkey reproduces monkeys and a human reproduces humans. So when God gives birth, what do you think He'll reproduce? gods, of course!

When God created Man, He created him in His image and after His likeness. That's why we look like Him; we have two hands the same way He has two hands. We have two legs, one head, one mouth, one nose, two ears and two eyes just like Him.

When someone gives his heart to Christ and becomes born again, he receives the divine nature. His spirit is imparted with the eternal life of Almighty God and he becomes one like Him – His very offspring. The Bible says in **James 1:18, "Of his own will begat he us with the word of truth..."** and in **1 Peter 1:23, "Being born again, not of corruptible seed, but of incorruptible, by the word of God, which liveth and abideth for ever."**

The Bible also says, **"Therefore if any man be in Christ, he is a new creature: old things are passed away; behold, all things are become new"** (2 **Corinthians 5:17**), Hallelujah!

Now that we're born again and partakers of His

divine nature (2 Peter 1:4), the life of God has taken up residence in our spirits. We're not what we used to be; we may look the same way we used to look on the outside, but on the inside, we're new creatures, born again and filled with the Spirit of God!

When God gives birth, you can't expect Him to produce a failure. That's inconsistent with His nature.

"Pastor Chris, are you saying we are gods?"

Well, I'm not the one who said it; God Himself said so in His Word: **"I have said ye are gods; and all of you are children of the most high (Psalm 82:6).** If God gave birth to you, what do you think you are? You must be a god under Him! He's Papa God, and we're His kids. Children of God ought to be gods. Come to think of it, if you can change the circumstances of your life, you must be a god! So God is training us just as a daddy trains his kids, because we belong to Him.

He wants us to understand the anointing that we have received and how it operates. Then we'll be able to take full advantage of it to cause the desired changes in our lives and circumstances.

Chapter Five

He Will Teach You All Things

When the Holy Spirit comes into your life, He becomes your Teacher who teaches you from the inside. The Psalmist declares in **Psalm 119:98, "Thou through thy commandments hast made me wiser than mine enemies..."**

David was talking about God the Holy Spirit and what He was able to accomplish in his life through the Word of God. He said the Holy Spirit, through His commandments, had made him wiser than his enemies. Then he went on to say, **"...for they** (His commandments) **are ever with me. I have more understanding than all my teachers: for thy testimonies are my meditation. I understand more than the ancients, because I keep thy precepts"** (Psalm 119:98-100).

He's letting you know the Holy Spirit can make you wiser than the ancients (wise old men) and even your enemies. He'll do it by teaching you from within. He'll show you the secrets of life and tell you what to do. He'll guide you from within and make you wiser than others around you.

Here's what Jesus said about the Holy Spirit in **John 14:26:**

> *"But the Comforter, which is the Holy Ghost, whom the Father will send in my name, he shall teach you all things, and bring all things to your remembrance..."*

This is wonderful! It means you'll no longer be

called a fool, because the Holy Spirit will teach you all things. He's not only going to teach you things in the Bible, but also all the things about life. He's already given you understanding. He's anointed you; now He's your Teacher, glory to God! No one can call you a fool anymore, because you have a Teacher inside you Who teaches you all things. If you listen to Him, He'll show you what to do.

Let me show you a very important verse in the Bible:

Psalm 16:11:

> *"Thou wilt shew me the path of life: in thy presence is fulness of joy; at thy right hand there are pleasures for ever- more."*

As your Teacher, the Holy Spirit will show you the path of life. By yourself you do not and cannot know the path of life. The Bible says in **Proverbs 14:12, "There is a way which seemeth right unto a man, but the end thereof are the ways of death."** The way that seems right to you ends up in death and destruction, but when the Holy Spirit takes over your life, He'll show you the path of life, glory to God!

Isaiah 48:17:

"Thus saith the Lord, thy Redeemer, the Holy One of Israel; I am the Lord thy God which teacheth thee to profit, which leadeth thee by the way that thou shouldest go."

With the Holy Spirit, you have it made! For you, life is already successful. He knows something more about your profession than you will ever know. He knows about your business better than you do. He knows all about your family and He can help you build a wonderful family. He can help you train up your kids. There are parents who are literally running mad because of their children, but the Holy Ghost can help you. He can teach you how to train those kids. He can teach you anything!

The trouble with too many of us is that we're not

taking advantage of His presence in our lives. For example, you want to make more money on your job or in your business, but you don't know how. No, you don't have to lie and cheat to get ahead in that job or business. The Holy Spirit can show you exactly what to do. He can teach you how to make wealth and you'll stop losing money or making the wrong investments.

Maybe your health has been unstable; the Holy Spirit will teach you how to stay in health. You may be concerned about your size; maybe you're too slim or too fat. The Holy Spirit can show you what to do. He can teach you all things, and He's asking, "What do you want?"

You have a Teacher in you. He lives in you and He can teach you anything. Why then should you be confused? That shouldn't be your lot. You have a Teacher Who knows all things, and because He lives in you and teaches you all things, you're intelligent. What's more, He's able to remind you whatever He teaches you. That's why I say you have super-intelligence!

Someone says, "Well, I don't know anything. I just have a little brain and I can't even think straight."

That's an insult to the Spirit of God. The Bible says we have not received the spirit of timidity or cowardice but of power, of love and of a sound mind (2 Timothy 1:7). You have a sound mind, glory to God!

People from our city—Zion—are not easily accepted in this world. A lot of times, the world doesn't understand the language we speak. They think we're proud and braggadocious. But we just can't talk like them. We can't say, "I'm poor" or "I'm just average." No Sir, we couldn't be! We know who we are—We're rich, we're excellent, we're powerful and influencial because we've got the Holy Ghost on the inside. He is the One Who illuminates our minds and teaches us wondrous things from God's Word, Hallelujah!

Chapter Six

He Will Guide You

The man without the Holy Spirit is like sheep without a shepherd; an aircraft without a pilot; a ship lost at sea, without a captain. The man without the Holy Spirit is a man walking in darkness. He's lost and without a sense of direction, until the Holy Spirit comes into his life.

The Holy Spirit is the Ultimate Guide. When He comes to live in you, not only does He teach you, He also guides you in the affairs of life. Jesus showed us this in **John 16:13** when He said,

> *"Howbeit when he, the Spirit of truth, is come, he will guide you into all truth: for he shall not speak of himself; but whatsoever he shall hear, that shall he speak: and he will shew you things to come."*

You will no longer be deceived, for the Holy Spirit will guide you into all truth – He will guide you into all reality. Someone may deceive you for a short time, but he cannot completely deceive you for too long. Why? The Holy Spirit in your life will guide you, He will show you what is real.

This is something He does inside you. He guides and leads you from within. The Bible says, **"For as many as are led by the Spirit of God, they are the sons of God" (Romans 8:14).** Just to think about this is exciting. Do you remember how God brought the children of Israel out of Egypt? Let's read how David recounts it:

Psalm 105:7:

"He brought them forth also with sil-ver and gold: and there was not one feeble person among their tribes."

Can you imagine this! No grandma had to be supported by her son. No grandpa had to be carried by anybody. Everybody was strong enough to carry his own stuff and move on his own. This is the testimony of God – He brought them forth with silver and gold and there was not one feeble person among their tribes. This is talking about financial prosperity and health. Nobody was broke, nobody had a stroke. There wasn't anybody who was paralysed or impotent.

Let's read **verse 38:**

"Egypt was glad when they departed: for the fear of them fell upon them."

Wow! The Egyptians were so afraid of the children of Israel, they gave them everything of value they had and quickly sent them on their way. Boy, how so relieved they were to see them leave their land!

I tell you it's going to be the same way in the last days. Don't you ever think that when Jesus shows up at the rapture, we'll be escaping from here, saying, "Phew, thank You Jesus, we're out of that place!" No, sir! We're not going to be escaping from here. We're not going to be delivered from here at the rapture. Why, we would have lived so victoriously and subdued and dealt with this world to the extent that there won't be any reason for us to be here anymore!

Mark my words, we don't have too many years left to do that! That's the reason for the teaching of the Word of God. That's why God is bringing you this message. I've known and lived by the truths I'm sharing with you in this book for many years. Now, through the Spirit, God has allowed me share them with you, and that's because the time is short!

What you ought to do now is take up this message, stand by it, use it and begin to live in victory.

Let's look at some more of David's account of

Israel's departure from Egypt:

Psalm 105:38-45:

"Egypt was glad when they departed: for the fear of them fell upon them. He spread a 'cloud' for a covering; and 'fire' to give light in the night. The people asked, and he brought quails, and satisfied them with the bread of heaven. He opened the rock, and the waters gushed out; they ran in the dry places like a river. For he remembered his holy promise, and Abraham his servant. And he brought forth his people with joy, and his chosen with gladness: And gave them the lands of the heathen: and they inherited the labour of the people; That they might observe his statutes, and keep his laws. Praise ye the Lord."

The 'cloud' and the 'fire' refer to the Holy Ghost, and this whole passage shows us how He guarded and guided the Israelites throughout their sojourn in the wilderness. He provided for them and protected them against all their enemies.

That was back in the Old Testament. How much more does God, through His Holy Spirit, help and bless us today who are partakers of the New Covenant. You see, you're a blessed person. In your office, the results you get ought to be greater than the results of the ordinary man. Your results ought to be blessed. The way you do things ought to be different; it ought to speak of excellence because there's a light shinning on your path and the Spirit of excellence dwells within you. You only have to make up your mind that that's the way it's going to be, and it's going to be just that way.

If you thought you had seen some increase in your life, you've not seen anything yet. Wait till you're through reading this book! Your life will never be the same again. As you begin to walk with this mighty Spirit of God I'm talking about and allow Him to operate in your life, you will experience supernatural peace, prosperity and great development in every area of your life.

When the Holy Spirit comes to live within you, He not only seals up the life of God that you've received (Ephesians 1:13; 4:30), He makes it work! He makes you a child of God in truth and reality and leads you on in this new life.

Romans 8:11 tells us He is "...the Spirit...that raised up Jesus from the dead..." Nobody was ever raised from the dead without a prophet praying for him. No one ever came out of the grave all by himself. But Jesus did through the power of the Holy Ghost! For three days and three nights, He was in the belly of the earth, and the Bible says He was raised from the dead by 'the glory of the Father.'

What, or rather, *who* is 'the glory of the Father'? It's the Holy Spirit! Remember, we read in Psalm 105 verse 39 that the children of Israel were covered with a cloud that led them in the daytime (see also Psalm 78:14). That 'glory cloud' was the Holy Spirit! So when Paul wrote in Romans 8:11 that Jesus was raised from the dead by 'the glory of the Father,' he was referring to the Holy Spirit. The Holy Spirit is the manifestation of the glory of God!

Chapter Seven

He Will Cause You To Do Right!

*T*here are people who take drugs, because when they do, they get high and feel they can do absolutely anything and even be superhuman. Sometimes some people get drunk and start staggering around, totally oblivious of where they are or what they're doing.

Well, let me tell you something, child of God: You don't need drugs; you don't need nicotine, cocaine, heroin, marijuana or alcohol. What you need is the

Holy Ghost! When the Holy Ghost takes over your spirit, your soul and your body, you're changed forever.

In **Ezekiel 36:27** the Bible says,

> *"And I will put my spirit within you, and cause you to walk in my statutes, and ye shall keep my judgments, and do them."*

In this Scripture, God is saying He will bring the Holy Ghost into your life, Who will give you the ability and capacity to obey Him and do His Will. You'll no longer struggle to please God or do right. You won't need to try to do His will anymore.

God said, "I will put My Spirit within you and cause you to do My will. I will cause you to obey My statutes, to walk in My statutes and follow My judgements." In other words, when you find yourself going in the street and the Holy Ghost suddenly says to you, "Stop! Turn left," you would have responded ever before you had the time to reason it out.

When the Holy Ghost comes i~~n~~ everything you do turns into success. You people don't understand how we're able ___ ~~d~~raw the large crowds that attend our services and crusades. They think it's the result of good pub-licity. No, it's not the publicity in itself that draws the crowds, it's the Holy Ghost! The publicity we do is anointed by the Holy Ghost. When we release handbills and invitation cards or put a promo on television to advertise a programme, they're anointed by the Holy Ghost.

So when we invite people, they're anointed by the same Holy Ghost, Who causes them to come. Many of them don't know why they're coming, but they all just keep coming. They come out of their homes, offices and shops, because of the Holy Ghost, glory to God!

Now let me tell you something: The same power of the Holy Ghost that pulls people into our meetings without many of them even knowing why they're coming will begin to pull success and favour into your life. Do you know why? It's because God loves people and loves to bless people. That's why He brought you into this world – to bless you and to favour you. That's why He gave you the Holy Ghost, Who causes you to do the right things that release the blessing and the favour of God upon your life. Glorrrrry yy!!!

Chapter Eight

He Will Bring Colour Into Your Life

When the Holy Ghost comes into you, He will bring colour and beauty into your life. Oh, how I wish I had a way to express this to you even more strongly! But let me repeat that so it can sink into your spirit: **If the Holy Ghost finds a vent in you, if He finds a way to express Himself in your life, He will bring beauty and favour into your life.**

Life is actually full of beauty. Life is full of joy. You can experience all the beauty and joy life has to offer.

Only let the Holy Spirit show you how. Some people think that if they're successful in business they'll be happy. Then, they become successful and they're still not happy. Some think that if they have a lot of money, they'll be happy, but when they get all the money they want, they're still unhappy.

Some others think that if they get married to a successful person they'll be happy, and then they get married to someone they think is successful and are still unhappy. Still some others think if they have children they'll be happy, then they have children but remain as unhappy as ever. So they say, "Alright, maybe I should build a house." They build a mansion and they're still unhappy!

Another thought occurs to them, "Maybe I should go back to school and get a better degree." They go to the best schools and obtain even more prestigious degrees than they had before but are still unhappy. They continually wonder about their lives and what they should do with it. They're in an endless but fruitless search for something that will make their lives more enjoyable and fulfilling.

If any of these describes you, I know just what, actually, *Who* you need. You need the Holy Spirit. The Holy Spirit is the beauty of God. The Bible says, **"By His Spirit the heavens He beautified..." (Job 26:13 Young's Literal Translation).** The beauty of God's creation was produced by the Holy Spirit.

> *"In the beginning God created the heaven and the earth. And the earth was without form, and void; and darkness was upon the face of the deep..."*
> **Genesis 1:1-2.**

In other words, the earth had become a chaotic mass, and darkness was upon the face of the deep. Then it goes on to tell us:

> *"...And the Spirit of God moved upon the face of the waters"* Verse 2.

There was darkness in the earth; it was formless and empty, but as the Spirit of God began to move over that darkness and emptiness, as He brooded upon it, the Bible says,

"And God said, Let there be light: and there was light" Genesis 1:3.

Here's what happened: When God said, "Let there be light," the Holy Spirit swung into action (remember, all this time He had been brooding upon the face of the waters) and brought forth light!

If there's darkness in your life; if your life is formless and colourless, and you've been wondering what to do with it; if you've been struggling so hard to make something out of your life, it's time to quit struggling! The Lord Jesus said,

"Come unto me, all ye that labour **(struggle)** *and are heavy laden* **(saddled with a lot of burden),** *and I will give you rest"* **(Matthew 11:28).**

Jesus says to you today, "I know what you're looking for, and I'll give it to you. Come and I will give you rest from your struggles, wars and frustrations." Hallelujah!

The Holy Ghost has brought so much beauty into my life. I'm full of the Holy Ghost. What a life it is with the Holy Ghost! Oh, how I wish you could see the life you should be living with the Holy Spirit. If you have the Holy Spirit dwelling in you, He'll bring the beauty of God into your heart and your life. Your life will be so full of colour that those around you will begin to wonder what you're doing that makes you so special.

Remember, He made King David's life so beautiful, he had to declare, "God, You've made me a wonder to my generation!" (Psalm 71:7). The Holy Ghost wants to make you a wonder to your generation; He wants to make you a wonder to your world. Let Him take His place in your life and He'll bring in all of His glory and beauty.

This is the sixth thing the Holy Spirit will do in your life – to bring colour and beauty into your life. Isaiah said He'll give you beauty for ashes (Isaiah 61:3). Instead of shame, there'll be beauty in your life. People will look at you and see the favour of God upon your life, because of the Holy Spirit.

The Bible says about Jesus that He was full of grace and truth (John 1:14). Jesus was full of grace. <u>Grace is the beauty of God that flows from the inside and can be seen on the outside.</u> It resides in you. <u>That's what the Holy Spirit brings into your life in overflowing measure when you let Him have His place in you.</u>

Chapter Nine

He Will Vitalize Your Mortal Body

And if Christ be in you, (though) the body is dead because of sin; but the Spirit is life (the Holy Spirit gives it life), because of righteousness. But if the Spirit of him that raised up Jesus from the dead dwell in you, he that raised up Christ from the dead shall also quicken (vitalize) your mortal bodies by his Spirit that dwelleth in *you"* (**Romans 8:10-11**).

Paul the apostle said, "If the Spirit of Him that raised Jesus from the dead lives in you, that same Spirit will vitalize your mortal body. Even if your body had been paralysed, if the Spirit of Him that raised Jesus from the dead comes to dwell in you, He will drive away the paralysis and vitalize your body."

It is our gain for us to possess the Holy Spirit

If that same Spirit that raised Jesus from the dead lives in you, He will destroy the cancer. He will get rid of the tumour and drive every demon out of your body! If that Spirit dwells in your body, the HIV will leave; the diabetes will die. The deaf ears will be unstopped and the blindness will go, becasue He will vitalize your mortal body, Hallelujah!

That's why I'm telling you your suffering is unnecessary. Your poverty is unnecessary. Your struggling is unnecessary. You don't need to struggle or suffer anymore. You don't need to be poor anymore. If that same Spirit lives in you, He will make you a success.

Back in the days of the early Church recorded in the Scriptures, it was so important for people to receive the Holy Spirit. I wonder why so many Christians today seem not to care a hoot about the Holy Ghost. Many who have received Him don't even know Who He is.

But thank God, through this book, you're discovering Who the Holy Spirit is and what He will do when He comes into your life. One of the things the Spirit of God will do in your life when He comes to live in you is to bring the fire and the glory of God into your life, and to vitalize your mortal body.

"STAND UPRIGHT ON THY FEET!"

Acts 14:8-11: *"And there sat a certain man at Lystra, impotent in his feet, being a cripple from his mother's womb, who never had walked: The same heard Paul speak: who stedfastly beholding him, and perceiving that he had faith to be healed, Said with a loud voice, Stand upright on thy feet.*

And he leaped and walked. And when the people saw what Paul had done, they lifted up their voices, saying in the speech of Lycaonia, The gods are come down to us in the likeness of men."

In this portion of Scripture, Paul was preaching at Lystra, and while he was preaching, there was a man listening to him, who was impotent in his feet and had never walked from birth. He sat there listening intently as Paul preached this same message of the regenerating power of the Holy Spirit that I'm sharing with you. When he heard it, he believed it, and Paul looked at him and said, "Man, stand up!" Right away, the cripple sprang up on his feet and began to walk! Paul didn't have to pray for him.

You see, if you're a child of God and you have the Holy Ghost, you don't need to be prayed for anymore. You have the eternal life of Almighty God travelling through your veins and the indwelling presence of His Spirit. That's all you need to overcome the devil, sickness, disease and infirmity.

The Bible says in **John 1:12-13, "But as many as received him, to them gave he power to become the sons of God, even to them that believe on his name:Which were born, not of blood, nor of the will of the flesh, nor of the will of man, but of God."** This is the reason sickness shouldn't be able to travel through your body when you're born again, because your life is no longer the life of blood!

In Leviticus 17:11, the Bible says the life of the flesh is in the blood, but when you're born again, the life of your body is no longer in your blood but in your spirit.

Remember **Romans 8:11** says, **"But if the Spirit of him that raised up Jesus from the dead dwell in you, he that raised up Christ from the dead shall also quicken your mortal bodies by his Spirit that dwelleth in you."** That same Spirit that raised Christ from the dead dwells in you and He gives life to your mortal body. So you do not live by blood anymore, but by the power of the Holy Ghost Who strenghtens, energizes and gives life to your physical body.

Chapter Ten

A Final Word

I have some very important questions to ask you as you read through the few pages remaining in this book:

Why should you continue in your situation after having read this book? Why should you continue to suffer the way you do? Why should your life still be full of struggles?

You may have been struggling all your life.

Everything you have in your life may have come to you through much toil and struggle. You may even have thought before reading this book that it's impossible to receive anything worthwhile without struggling for it.

I'm sure the message in this book has changed your perception and changed your life. Why, the Holy Spirit is the best gift we ever received from God and we got Him free of charge, without any struggles!

There are two types of people in the world – those who struggle through life and those who walk through life in blessing. The latter receive a blessing, such as is released through the message in this book, and their lives are changed. The former continue to struggle because they miss out on the message and the blessing conveyed in it. You must refuse to be a struggler or sufferer. God sent His Holy Spirit to you so you won't have to struggle or suffer in your life.

Remember, Jesus said, "...ye shall receive power, after that the Holy Ghost is come upon you." When you receive the Holy Spirit, you receive the power or 'dynamic ability to cause changes.' This means you can change anything! There's nothing you can't do when you're full of the Holy Ghost. With Him, you won't have to struggle through life anymore; and you won't have to be frustrated anymore, glory to God!

LET THE SPIRIT ACT ON THE WORD

God never does anything without His Word. Don't ever forget that. His Word is the foundation for everything. The Bible tells us in Genesis 1:1 that in the beginning God created the heaven and the earth, the earth was without form and void and the Spirit of God moved over the face of the waters. But even though the Spirit of God was present, nothing changed until God spoke His Word and said, "Let there be light!"

It was when God started speaking that the Spirit of God went to work to bring His Word to pass. The Holy Spirit acts on the Word of God to bring it to pass. That's why when God speaks, you must receive His Word. When you do, then the Holy Spirit acts on the

Word of God in your life to bring it to pass. He will make the Word good in your life and you'll have the results it speaks of.

GET FILLED WITH THE SPIRIT!

Ephesians 3:17-18:

"That Christ may dwell in your hearts by faith; that ye, being rooted and grounded in love, May be able to comprehend with all saints what is the breadth, and length, and depth, and height; And to know the love of Christ, which passeth knowledge, that ye might be filled with all the fulness of God."

Ephesians 5:18:

"And be not drunk with wine, wherein is excess; but be filled with the Spirit;"

In Ephesians chapter five and verse eighteen, we're instructed not to be drunk with wine wherein is

70

excess but be filled with the Holy Ghost. Now, that's talking along the same lines as the eighteenth verse of the third chapter where it says, **"that ye might be filled with the fullness of God."**

God wants us filled with all of His fullness. This is what is really meant by being filled with the Spirit. It means to be filled with the fullness of God. It's one thing to have God, it's another thing to be filled with His fullness. To be filled with His fullness means to be filled with His completeness.

For the Holy Spirit to live in a man means for that man to have all of the life and nature of God in him. When the Holy Spirit indwells a human person, He makes him uncon-querable, indomitable! He makes him more than a man. He infuses his humanity with the life and power of Divinity. This is what changes a man completely.

Joel, the Old Testament prophet foretold:

> *"And it shall come to pass afterward, that I will pour out my spirit upon all*

flesh; and your sons and your daugh-
ters shall prophesy, your old men shall
dream dreams, your young men shall
see visions: And also upon the servants
and upon the handmaids in those days
will I pour out my spirit"
(Joel 2:28-29).

When he said, "Your sons and your daughters shall prophesy," he meant they shall speak 'words of power.' In other words, what they say shall come to pass. When you're filled with the Holy Spirit, your words cease to be the words of men; they become anointed with power.

When the Spirit of God is working in you and you're overflowing with His fullness, you won't need to try to muster boldness to say or do things. You won't need to try to stir up some boldness or remember some Scriptures in the face of adversity. No! The life you have when you're filled with the Holy Spirit is the life of boldness, it's the life of dominion over all circumstances.

The Holy Spirit has told
because He is with us (Jeremiah
us. He dwells in us that we might k
fullness of God. You ought to have H
such that when you move, it's the Spiri   .ather
moving in you. Then, your hands become His hands
and your fingers His fingers. He sees through your eyes,
talks through your mouth and moves with your body.
That's what He seeks to do in your life today.

Remember that you're not of this world. You have
something the prophets and priests of old did not have.
You have the capacity to contain the fullness of God's
Spirit!

Ephesians 5:18-20:

*"And be not drunk with wine, wherein
is excess; but be filled with the Spirit;
Speaking to yourselves in psalms and
hymns and spiritual songs, singing and
making melody in your heart to the
Lord; Giving thanks always for all*

things unto God and the Father in the name of our Lord Jesus Christ;"

From this Scripture, we see the blueprint for getting filled with the Holy Spirit. If you want to be filled with the Holy Spirit and experience in your life these seven vital blessings that He brings, then you need to start speaking to yourself in psalms and hymns and spiritual songs. You've got to start singing and making melody in your heart to the Lord. You've got to give thanks to God the Father always for all things, in the Name of Jesus.

For example, you could begin to thank God by saying to Him, "Lord, I'm so blessed. I don't know how to say it enough but You've blessed me so much, I'm embarrassed! I look into Your Word and I find out you've blessed me. Then I look at my life and I see that I'm really, truly blessed. Thank You Lord Jesus!"

By the time you're confessing God's Word and giving Him thanks like this, you'll begin to feel the anointing welling up so strongly within you and the power of the Holy Ghost will come all over you.

74

That's the way I pray, for that's the way He told us to pray. Sometimes I say to Him, "Lord, You told us to be filled with the Spirit, speaking to ourselves in psalms and hymns and spiritual songs. Lord, I'm going to make You some psalms, and sing You some hymns now..." And when I start doing that, I get full of God's Spirit, Hallelujah!

It's time for you to be filled with the Spirit. Go ahead and start praying and singing in the Holy Ghost. Start laughing and dancing in the Spirit. Start praising God and rejoicing in His presence, for in His presence there's fullness of joy. Don't wait, get in the flow! God's Spirit is working right now and you can get so filled with the Holy Ghost, you'll be drunk with Him! Thank God for these seven things the Holy Spirit will do in you as you walk with Him daily.

To contact the author write:
Pastor Chris Oyakhilome:

United Kingdom:
Christ Embassy Int'l Office
Loveworld Conference Centre
Cheriton High Street
Folkestone, Kent CT19 4QJ
Tel:+44(0)1303 270970
Fax:01303 274 372

South Africa:
303 Pretoria Avenue
Cnr. Harley and Bram Fischer,
Randburg, Gauteng
South Africa.
Tel: + 27 11 3260971;
+27 113260972

Nigeria:
Christ Embassy Church
P.O. Box 13563, Ikeja,
Lagos, Nigeria.
Tel:+234-8023324188
+234-8052464131; +234-1-8925724

or email:pastorchris@christembassy.org

Please include your testimony or help received from
this book when you write.
Your prayer requests are also welcome.

Reaching out with the gospel. Building up the saints
with excellence and clarity.